This Quilt
Journal Belongs
to

Michelle Binkowski ♥

Reference and Conversions

Most quilt fabrics come in widths of 45 inches (1 and 1/4 yards) of which about 42 inches is usable

Yard	Inches
1/8	4.5
1/4	9
1/3	12
1/2	18
2/3	24
3/4	27
1	36
1 1/2	54
2	72

Fraction	Decimal
1/16	.0625
1/8	.125
3/16	.1875
1/4	.25
5/16	.3125
1/3	.333
3/8	.375
7/16	.4375
1/2	.5
9/16	.5625
5/8	.625
2/3	.666
11/16	.6875
3/4	.75
13/16	.8125
7/8	.875
15/16	.9375

Typical U.S. bed sizes

Bed	Dimensions	Standard Bedding Sizes	Quilt with 16" overlap per side
Crib	28" X 52"	45" X 60"	60" X 84"
Twin	39" X 75"	72" X 90"	71" X 107"
Full (Double)	54" X 75"	81" X 96"	85" X 107"
Queen	60" X 80"	90" X 108"	92" X 112"
King	76" X 80"	120" X 120"	108" X 112"

Resources

Websites

_____

_____

_____

_____

_____

_____

_____

Magazines and Catalogs

_____

_____

_____

_____

_____

_____

_____

Other

_____

_____

_____

_____

_____

_____

_____

Quilt Project Plan

Date _2·21·2022_

Quilt is for: Me ___✓___ To Gift _____ To Sell _____
              & Ms. Laurie
Recipient, if a gift:_____

Size of quilt:
Baby ___ Lap ✓ Twin ___ Queen ___ King ___ Other _____

Pattern name: _Lonestar/Star quilt (Supernova)_

Colors to use: _Supernova Rainbow Star w/deep dark_
             celestial/batique inspired colors.
Pattern to use: _Star Quilt Pattern for a Lakota single star_

Type of batting: _regular quilt batting_

How it will be quilted:
By Hand _✓_____ a combo
By Machine _✓____ By me
By Someone Else _____

Notes

The inspiration comes from always wanting my own
Lonestar quilt to display on the sofa in our
main living place in deep rich jewel/Rainbow
colors. Then I found a tote bag with the image
of a fantastic star quilt called "Supernova"
That I have absolutely fallen in love with!

Quilt Project Plan - Materials

Fabric
Top

_____

_____

_____

_____

Backing

_Celestial_____

_____

Binding

_Dark star print (coordinating)_____

Thread

Color _____
Size & Number of Spools _____

Color _____
Size & Number of Spools _____

Color _____
Size & Number of Spools _____

Batting

Size _____
Loft _____
Cotton/Wool/Bamboo/Blend _____

Other Materials

_____

_____

_____

_____

_____

_____

Yardage and Fabric Swatches

Name of fabric _____

Manufacturer _____

Cost per yard _____

Date purchased _____

Notes _____

_____

Name of fabric _____

Manufacturer _____

Cost per yard _____

Date purchased _____

Notes _____

_____

Name of fabric _____

Manufacturer _____

Cost per yard _____

Date purchased _____

Notes _____

_____

Yardage and Fabric Swatches

Name of fabric

Manufacturer

Cost per yard

Date purchased

Notes

Name of fabric

Manufacturer

Cost per yard

Date purchased

Notes

Name of fabric

Manufacturer

Cost per yard

Date purchased

Notes

Yardage and Fabric Swatches

Name of fabric _____

Manufacturer _____

Cost per yard _____

Date purchased _____

Notes _____

_____

Name of fabric _____

Manufacturer _____

Cost per yard _____

Date purchased _____

Notes _____

_____

Name of fabric _____

Manufacturer _____

Cost per yard _____

Date purchased _____

Notes _____

_____

Yardage and Fabric Swatches

Name of fabric

Manufacturer

Cost per yard

Date purchased

Notes

Name of fabric

Manufacturer

Cost per yard

Date purchased

Notes

Name of fabric

Manufacturer

Cost per yard

Date purchased

Notes

Yardage and Fabric Swatches

Name of fabric _____

Manufacturer _____

Cost per yard _____

Date purchased _____

Notes _____

_____

Name of fabric _____

Manufacturer _____

Cost per yard _____

Date purchased _____

Notes _____

_____

Name of fabric _____

Manufacturer _____

Cost per yard _____

Date purchased _____

Notes _____

_____

Yardage and Fabric Swatches

Name of fabric _____

Manufacturer _____

Cost per yard _____

Date purchased _____

Notes _____

_____

Name of fabric _____

Manufacturer _____

Cost per yard _____

Date purchased _____

Notes _____

_____

Name of fabric _____

Manufacturer _____

Cost per yard _____

Date purchased _____

Notes _____

_____

Quilt Project Plan

Date _____

Quilt is for: Me _____ To Gift _____ To Sell _____

Recipient, if a gift:_____

Size of quilt:
Baby ____ Lap ____ Twin ____ Queen ____ King ____ Other _____

Pattern name: _____

Colors to use:_____

Pattern to use: _____

Type of batting: _____

How it will be quilted:
By Hand _____
By Machine _____
By Someone Else _____

Notes

_____

_____

_____

_____

_____

_____

_____

Quilt Project Plan - Materials

Fabric

Top

_____

_____

_____

_____

Backing

_____

_____

Binding

_____

Thread

Color _____

Size & Number of Spools _____

Color _____

Size & Number of Spools _____

Color _____

Size & Number of Spools _____

Batting

Size _____

Loft _____

Cotton/Wool/Bamboo/Blend _____

Other Materials

_____

_____

_____

_____

_____

Yardage and Fabric Swatches

Name of fabric _____

Manufacturer _____

Cost per yard _____

Date purchased _____

Notes _____

_____

Name of fabric _____

Manufacturer _____

Cost per yard _____

Date purchased _____

Notes _____

_____

Name of fabric _____

Manufacturer _____

Cost per yard _____

Date purchased _____

Notes _____

_____

Yardage and Fabric Swatches

Name of fabric ....

Manufacturer ....

Cost per yard ....

Date purchased ....

Notes ....

....

Name of fabric ....

Manufacturer ....

Cost per yard ....

Date purchased ....

Notes ....

Name of fabric ....

Manufacturer ....

Cost per yard ....

Date purchased ....

Notes ....

....

Yardage and Fabric Swatches

Name of fabric _____

Manufacturer _____

Cost per yard _____

Date purchased _____

Notes _____

_____

Name of fabric _____

Manufacturer _____

Cost per yard _____

Date purchased _____

Notes _____

_____

Name of fabric _____

Manufacturer _____

Cost per yard _____

Date purchased _____

Notes _____

_____

Yardage and Fabric Swatches

Name of fabric

Manufacturer

Cost per yard

Date purchased

Notes

Name of fabric

Manufacturer

Cost per yard

Date purchased

Notes

Name of fabric

Manufacturer

Cost per yard

Date purchased

Notes

Yardage and Fabric Swatches

Name of fabric _____

Manufacturer _____

Cost per yard _____

Date purchased _____

Notes _____

_____

Name of fabric _____

Manufacturer _____

Cost per yard _____

Date purchased _____

Notes _____

Name of fabric _____

Manufacturer _____

Cost per yard _____

Date purchased _____

Notes _____

Yardage and Fabric Swatches

Name of fabric ....

Manufacturer ....

Cost per yard ....

Date purchased ....

Notes ....

....

Name of fabric ....

Manufacturer ....

Cost per yard ....

Date purchased ....

Notes ....

....

Name of fabric ....

Manufacturer ....

Cost per yard ....

Date purchased ....

Notes ....

....

Quilt Project Plan

Date _____

Quilt is for: Me _____ To Gift _____ To Sell _____

Recipient, if a gift:_____

Size of quilt:
Baby ____ Lap ____ Twin ____ Queen ____ King ____ Other _____

Pattern name: _____

Colors to use:_____

Pattern to use: _____

Type of batting: _____

How it will be quilted:
By Hand _____
By Machine _____
By Someone Else _____

Notes

_____

_____

_____

_____

_____

_____

_____

Quilt Project Plan - Materials

Fabric

Top

_____

_____

_____

_____

_____

Backing

_____

_____

Binding

_____

Thread

Color _____

Size & Number of Spools _____

Color _____

Size & Number of Spools _____

Color _____

Size & Number of Spools _____

Batting

Size _____

Loft _____

Cotton/Wool/Bamboo/Blend _____

Other Materials

_____

_____

_____

_____

_____

_____

Yardage and Fabric Swatches

Name of fabric _____

Manufacturer _____

Cost per yard _____

Date purchased _____

Notes _____

_____

Name of fabric _____

Manufacturer _____

Cost per yard _____

Date purchased _____

Notes _____

_____

Name of fabric _____

Manufacturer _____

Cost per yard _____

Date purchased _____

Notes _____

_____

Yardage and Fabric Swatches

Name of fabric

Manufacturer

Cost per yard

Date purchased

Notes

Name of fabric

Manufacturer

Cost per yard

Date purchased

Notes

Name of fabric

Manufacturer

Cost per yard

Date purchased

Notes

Yardage and Fabric Swatches

Name of fabric _____

Manufacturer _____

Cost per yard _____

Date purchased _____

Notes _____

_____

Name of fabric _____

Manufacturer _____

Cost per yard _____

Date purchased _____

Notes _____

_____

Name of fabric _____

Manufacturer _____

Cost per yard _____

Date purchased _____

Notes _____

_____

Yardage and Fabric Swatches

Name of fabric _____

Manufacturer _____

Cost per yard _____

Date purchased _____

Notes _____

_____

Name of fabric _____

Manufacturer _____

Cost per yard _____

Date purchased _____

Notes _____

_____

Name of fabric _____

Manufacturer _____

Cost per yard _____

Date purchased _____

Notes _____

_____

Yardage and Fabric Swatches

Name of fabric _____

Manufacturer _____

Cost per yard _____

Date purchased _____

Notes _____

_____

Name of fabric _____

Manufacturer _____

Cost per yard _____

Date purchased _____

Notes _____

_____

Name of fabric _____

Manufacturer _____

Cost per yard _____

Date purchased _____

Notes _____

_____

Yardage and Fabric Swatches

Name of fabric _____

Manufacturer _____

Cost per yard _____

Date purchased _____

Notes _____

_____

Name of fabric _____

Manufacturer _____

Cost per yard _____

Date purchased _____

Notes _____

_____

Name of fabric _____

Manufacturer _____

Cost per yard _____

Date purchased _____

Notes _____

_____

Quilt Project Plan

Date _____

Quilt is for: Me _____ To Gift _____ To Sell _____

Recipient, if a gift:_____

Size of quilt:
Baby ____ Lap ____ Twin ____ Queen ____ King ____ Other _____

Pattern name: _____

Colors to use:_____

Pattern to use: _____

Type of batting: _____

How it will be quilted:
By Hand _____
By Machine _____
By Someone Else _____

Notes

_____

_____

_____

_____

_____

_____

_____

Quilt Project Plan - Materials

Fabric
Top

_____

_____

_____

_____

_____

Backing

_____

_____

Binding

_____

Thread

Color _____

Size & Number of Spools _____

Color _____

Size & Number of Spools _____

Color _____

Size & Number of Spools _____

Batting

Size _____

Loft _____

Cotton/Wool/Bamboo/Blend _____

Other Materials

_____

_____

_____

_____

_____

_____

Yardage and Fabric Swatches

Name of fabric _____

Manufacturer _____

Cost per yard _____

Date purchased _____

Notes _____

_____

Name of fabric _____

Manufacturer _____

Cost per yard _____

Date purchased _____

Notes _____

_____

Name of fabric _____

Manufacturer _____

Cost per yard _____

Date purchased _____

Notes _____

_____

Yardage and Fabric Swatches

Name of fabric _____

Manufacturer _____

Cost per yard _____

Date purchased _____

Notes _____

_____

Name of fabric _____

Manufacturer _____

Cost per yard _____

Date purchased _____

Notes _____

_____

Name of fabric _____

Manufacturer _____

Cost per yard _____

Date purchased _____

Notes _____

_____

Yardage and Fabric Swatches

Name of fabric _____

Manufacturer _____

Cost per yard _____

Date purchased _____

Notes _____

_____

Name of fabric _____

Manufacturer _____

Cost per yard _____

Date purchased _____

Notes _____

_____

Name of fabric _____

Manufacturer _____

Cost per yard _____

Date purchased _____

Notes _____

_____

Yardage and Fabric Swatches

Name of fabric

Manufacturer

Cost per yard

Date purchased

Notes

Name of fabric

Manufacturer

Cost per yard

Date purchased

Notes

Name of fabric

Manufacturer

Cost per yard

Date purchased

Notes

Yardage and Fabric Swatches

Name of fabric _____

Manufacturer _____

Cost per yard _____

Date purchased _____

Notes _____

_____

Name of fabric _____

Manufacturer _____

Cost per yard _____

Date purchased _____

Notes _____

_____

Name of fabric _____

Manufacturer _____

Cost per yard _____

Date purchased _____

Notes _____

_____

Yardage and Fabric Swatches

Name of fabric

Manufacturer

Cost per yard

Date purchased

Notes

Name of fabric

Manufacturer

Cost per yard

Date purchased

Notes

Name of fabric

Manufacturer

Cost per yard

Date purchased

Notes

Quilt Project Plan

Date _____

Quilt is for: Me _____ To Gift _____ To Sell _____

Recipient, if a gift:_____

Size of quilt:
Baby ____ Lap ____ Twin ____ Queen ____ King ____ Other _____

Pattern name: _____

Colors to use:_____

Pattern to use: _____

Type of batting: _____

How it will be quilted:
By Hand _____
By Machine _____
By Someone Else _____

Notes

_____

_____

_____

_____

_____

_____

_____

Quilt Project Plan - Materials

Fabric

Top

_____
_____
_____
_____
_____

Backing

_____
_____

Binding

_____

Thread

Color _____
Size & Number of Spools _____

Color _____
Size & Number of Spools _____

Color _____
Size & Number of Spools _____

Batting

Size _____
Loft _____
Cotton/Wool/Bamboo/Blend _____

Other Materials

_____
_____
_____
_____
_____
_____

Yardage and Fabric Swatches

Name of fabric _____

Manufacturer _____

Cost per yard _____

Date purchased _____

Notes _____

_____

Name of fabric _____

Manufacturer _____

Cost per yard _____

Date purchased _____

Notes _____

_____

Name of fabric _____

Manufacturer _____

Cost per yard _____

Date purchased _____

Notes _____

_____

Yardage and Fabric Swatches

Name of fabric _____

Manufacturer _____

Cost per yard _____

Date purchased _____

Notes _____
_____

Name of fabric _____

Manufacturer _____

Cost per yard _____

Date purchased _____

Notes _____
_____

Name of fabric _____

Manufacturer _____

Cost per yard _____

Date purchased _____

Notes _____
_____

Yardage and Fabric Swatches

Name of fabric _____

Manufacturer _____

Cost per yard _____

Date purchased _____

Notes _____

_____

Name of fabric _____

Manufacturer _____

Cost per yard _____

Date purchased _____

Notes _____

_____

Name of fabric _____

Manufacturer _____

Cost per yard _____

Date purchased _____

Notes _____

_____

Yardage and Fabric Swatches

Name of fabric

Manufacturer

Cost per yard

Date purchased

Notes

Name of fabric

Manufacturer

Cost per yard

Date purchased

Notes

Name of fabric

Manufacturer

Cost per yard

Date purchased

Notes

Yardage and Fabric Swatches

Name of fabric _____

Manufacturer _____

Cost per yard _____

Date purchased _____

Notes _____

_____

Name of fabric _____

Manufacturer _____

Cost per yard _____

Date purchased _____

Notes _____

_____

Name of fabric _____

Manufacturer _____

Cost per yard _____

Date purchased _____

Notes _____

_____

Yardage and Fabric Swatches

Name of fabric

Manufacturer

Cost per yard

Date purchased

Notes

Name of fabric

Manufacturer

Cost per yard

Date purchased

Notes

Name of fabric

Manufacturer

Cost per yard

Date purchased

Notes

Quilt Project Plan

Date _____

Quilt is for: Me _____ To Gift _____ To Sell _____

Recipient, if a gift:_____

Size of quilt:
Baby ____ Lap ____ Twin ____ Queen ____ King ____ Other _____

Pattern name: _____

Colors to use:_____

Pattern to use: _____

Type of batting: _____

How it will be quilted:
By Hand _____
By Machine _____
By Someone Else _____

Notes

_____

_____

_____

_____

_____

_____

_____

Quilt Project Plan - Materials

Fabric

Top

_____

_____

_____

_____

_____

Backing

_____

_____

Binding

_____

Thread

Color _____

Size & Number of Spools _____

Color _____

Size & Number of Spools _____

Color _____

Size & Number of Spools _____

Batting

Size _____

Loft _____

Cotton/Wool/Bamboo/Blend _____

Other Materials

_____

_____

_____

_____

_____

_____

Yardage and Fabric Swatches

Name of fabric ....

Manufacturer ....

Cost per yard ....

Date purchased ....

Notes ....

....

Name of fabric ....

Manufacturer ....

Cost per yard ....

Date purchased ....

Notes ....

....

Name of fabric ....

Manufacturer ....

Cost per yard ....

Date purchased ....

Notes ....

....

Yardage and Fabric Swatches

Name of fabric _____

Manufacturer _____

Cost per yard _____

Date purchased _____

Notes _____

_____

Name of fabric _____

Manufacturer _____

Cost per yard _____

Date purchased _____

Notes _____

_____

Name of fabric _____

Manufacturer _____

Cost per yard _____

Date purchased _____

Notes _____

_____

Yardage and Fabric Swatches

Name of fabric _____

Manufacturer _____

Cost per yard _____

Date purchased _____

Notes _____

_____

Name of fabric _____

Manufacturer _____

Cost per yard _____

Date purchased _____

Notes _____

_____

Name of fabric _____

Manufacturer _____

Cost per yard _____

Date purchased _____

Notes _____

_____

Yardage and Fabric Swatches

Name of fabric

Manufacturer

Cost per yard

Date purchased

Notes

Name of fabric

Manufacturer

Cost per yard

Date purchased

Notes

Name of fabric

Manufacturer

Cost per yard

Date purchased

Notes

Yardage and Fabric Swatches

Name of fabric _____

Manufacturer _____

Cost per yard _____

Date purchased _____

Notes _____

_____

Name of fabric _____

Manufacturer _____

Cost per yard _____

Date purchased _____

Notes _____

_____

Name of fabric _____

Manufacturer _____

Cost per yard _____

Date purchased _____

Notes _____

_____

Yardage and Fabric Swatches

Name of fabric _____

Manufacturer _____

Cost per yard _____

Date purchased _____

Notes _____

_____

Name of fabric _____

Manufacturer _____

Cost per yard _____

Date purchased _____

Notes _____

_____

Name of fabric _____

Manufacturer _____

Cost per yard _____

Date purchased _____

Notes _____

_____

Quilt Project Plan

Date _____

Quilt is for: Me _____ To Gift _____ To Sell _____

Recipient, if a gift:_____

Size of quilt:
Baby ___ Lap ___ Twin ___ Queen ___ King ___ Other _____

Pattern name: _____

Colors to use:_____

Pattern to use: _____

Type of batting: _____

How it will be quilted:
By Hand _____
By Machine _____
By Someone Else _____

Notes

_____

_____

_____

_____

_____

_____

_____

Quilt Project Plan - Materials

Fabric

Top

_____

_____

_____

_____

_____

Backing

_____

_____

Binding

_____

Thread

Color _____

Size & Number of Spools _____

Color _____

Size & Number of Spools _____

Color _____

Size & Number of Spools _____

Batting

Size _____

Loft _____

Cotton/Wool/Bamboo/Blend _____

Other Materials

_____

_____

_____

_____

_____

_____

Yardage and Fabric Swatches

Name of fabric _____

Manufacturer _____

Cost per yard _____

Date purchased _____

Notes _____

_____

Name of fabric _____

Manufacturer _____

Cost per yard _____

Date purchased _____

Notes _____

_____

Name of fabric _____

Manufacturer _____

Cost per yard _____

Date purchased _____

Notes _____

_____

Yardage and Fabric Swatches

Name of fabric

Manufacturer

Cost per yard

Date purchased

Notes

Name of fabric

Manufacturer

Cost per yard

Date purchased

Notes

Name of fabric

Manufacturer

Cost per yard

Date purchased

Notes

Yardage and Fabric Swatches

Name of fabric ....

Manufacturer ....

Cost per yard ....

Date purchased ....

Notes ....

....

Name of fabric ....

Manufacturer ....

Cost per yard ....

Date purchased ....

Notes ....

....

Name of fabric ....

Manufacturer ....

Cost per yard ....

Date purchased ....

Notes ....

....

Yardage and Fabric Swatches

Name of fabric _____

Manufacturer _____

Cost per yard _____

Date purchased _____

Notes _____

_____

Name of fabric _____

Manufacturer _____

Cost per yard _____

Date purchased _____

Notes _____

_____

Name of fabric _____

Manufacturer _____

Cost per yard _____

Date purchased _____

Notes _____

_____

Yardage and Fabric Swatches

Name of fabric _____

Manufacturer _____

Cost per yard _____

Date purchased _____

Notes _____

_____

Name of fabric _____

Manufacturer _____

Cost per yard _____

Date purchased _____

Notes _____

_____

Name of fabric _____

Manufacturer _____

Cost per yard _____

Date purchased _____

Notes _____

_____

Yardage and Fabric Swatches

Name of fabric _____

Manufacturer _____

Cost per yard _____

Date purchased _____

Notes _____

_____

Name of fabric _____

Manufacturer _____

Cost per yard _____

Date purchased _____

Notes _____

_____

Name of fabric _____

Manufacturer _____

Cost per yard _____

Date purchased _____

Notes _____

_____

Quilt Project Plan

Date _____

Quilt is for: Me _____ To Gift _____ To Sell _____

Recipient, if a gift:_____

Size of quilt:
Baby ___ Lap ___ Twin ___ Queen ___ King ___ Other _____

Pattern name: _____

Colors to use:_____

Pattern to use: _____

Type of batting: _____

How it will be quilted:
By Hand _____
By Machine _____
By Someone Else _____

Notes

_____

_____

_____

_____

_____

_____

_____

Quilt Project Plan - Materials

Fabric

Top

_____

_____

_____

_____

_____

Backing

_____

_____

Binding

_____

Thread

Color _____

Size & Number of Spools _____

Color _____

Size & Number of Spools _____

Color _____

Size & Number of Spools _____

Batting

Size _____

Loft _____

Cotton/Wool/Bamboo/Blend _____

Other Materials

_____

_____

_____

_____

_____

Yardage and Fabric Swatches

Name of fabric _____

Manufacturer _____

Cost per yard _____

Date purchased _____

Notes _____

_____

Name of fabric _____

Manufacturer _____

Cost per yard _____

Date purchased _____

Notes _____

_____

Name of fabric _____

Manufacturer _____

Cost per yard _____

Date purchased _____

Notes _____

_____

Yardage and Fabric Swatches

Name of fabric _____

Manufacturer _____

Cost per yard _____

Date purchased _____

Notes _____

_____

Name of fabric _____

Manufacturer _____

Cost per yard _____

Date purchased _____

Notes _____

_____

Name of fabric _____

Manufacturer _____

Cost per yard _____

Date purchased _____

Notes _____

_____

Yardage and Fabric Swatches

Name of fabric ....

Manufacturer ....

Cost per yard ....

Date purchased ....

Notes ....

....

Name of fabric ....

Manufacturer ....

Cost per yard ....

Date purchased ....

Notes ....

....

Name of fabric ....

Manufacturer ....

Cost per yard ....

Date purchased ....

Notes ....

....

Yardage and Fabric Swatches

Name of fabric

Manufacturer

Cost per yard

Date purchased

Notes

Name of fabric

Manufacturer

Cost per yard

Date purchased

Notes

Name of fabric

Manufacturer

Cost per yard

Date purchased

Notes

Yardage and Fabric Swatches

Name of fabric _____

Manufacturer _____

Cost per yard _____

Date purchased _____

Notes _____

_____

Name of fabric _____

Manufacturer _____

Cost per yard _____

Date purchased _____

Notes _____

_____

Name of fabric _____

Manufacturer _____

Cost per yard _____

Date purchased _____

Notes _____

_____

Yardage and Fabric Swatches

Name of fabric _____

Manufacturer _____

Cost per yard _____

Date purchased _____

Notes _____

_____

Name of fabric _____

Manufacturer _____

Cost per yard _____

Date purchased _____

Notes _____

_____

Name of fabric _____

Manufacturer _____

Cost per yard _____

Date purchased _____

Notes _____

_____

Quilt Project Plan

Date _____

Quilt is for: Me _____ To Gift _____ To Sell _____

Recipient, if a gift:_____

Size of quilt:
Baby ___ Lap ___ Twin ___ Queen ___ King ___ Other _____

Pattern name: _____

Colors to use:_____

Pattern to use: _____

Type of batting: _____

How it will be quilted:
By Hand _____
By Machine _____
By Someone Else _____

Notes

_____

_____

_____

_____

_____

_____

_____

Quilt Project Plan - Materials

Fabric
Top

_____

_____

_____

_____

Backing

_____

_____

Binding

_____

Thread

Color _____

Size & Number of Spools _____

Color _____

Size & Number of Spools _____

Color _____

Size & Number of Spools _____

Batting

Size _____

Loft _____

Cotton/Wool/Bamboo/Blend _____

Other Materials

_____

_____

_____

_____

_____

_____

Yardage and Fabric Swatches

Name of fabric _____

Manufacturer _____

Cost per yard _____

Date purchased _____

Notes _____

_____

Name of fabric _____

Manufacturer _____

Cost per yard _____

Date purchased _____

Notes _____

_____

Name of fabric _____

Manufacturer _____

Cost per yard _____

Date purchased _____

Notes _____

_____

Yardage and Fabric Swatches

Name of fabric _____

Manufacturer _____

Cost per yard _____

Date purchased _____

Notes _____

_____

Name of fabric _____

Manufacturer _____

Cost per yard _____

Date purchased _____

Notes _____

_____

Name of fabric _____

Manufacturer _____

Cost per yard _____

Date purchased _____

Notes _____

_____

Yardage and Fabric Swatches

Name of fabric _____

Manufacturer _____

Cost per yard _____

Date purchased _____

Notes _____

_____

Name of fabric _____

Manufacturer _____

Cost per yard _____

Date purchased _____

Notes _____

_____

Name of fabric _____

Manufacturer _____

Cost per yard _____

Date purchased _____

Notes _____

_____

Yardage and Fabric Swatches

Name of fabric

Manufacturer

Cost per yard

Date purchased

Notes

Name of fabric

Manufacturer

Cost per yard

Date purchased

Notes

Name of fabric

Manufacturer

Cost per yard

Date purchased

Notes

Yardage and Fabric Swatches

Name of fabric ⎯⎯⎯⎯⎯⎯⎯⎯⎯⎯⎯

Manufacturer ⎯⎯⎯⎯⎯⎯⎯⎯⎯⎯⎯

Cost per yard ⎯⎯⎯⎯⎯⎯⎯⎯⎯⎯⎯

Date purchased ⎯⎯⎯⎯⎯⎯⎯⎯⎯⎯

Notes ⎯⎯⎯⎯⎯⎯⎯⎯⎯⎯⎯

⎯⎯⎯⎯⎯⎯⎯⎯⎯⎯⎯⎯⎯⎯⎯⎯

Name of fabric ⎯⎯⎯⎯⎯⎯⎯⎯⎯⎯⎯

Manufacturer ⎯⎯⎯⎯⎯⎯⎯⎯⎯⎯⎯

Cost per yard ⎯⎯⎯⎯⎯⎯⎯⎯⎯⎯⎯

Date purchased ⎯⎯⎯⎯⎯⎯⎯⎯⎯⎯

Notes ⎯⎯⎯⎯⎯⎯⎯⎯⎯⎯⎯

⎯⎯⎯⎯⎯⎯⎯⎯⎯⎯⎯⎯⎯⎯⎯⎯

Name of fabric ⎯⎯⎯⎯⎯⎯⎯⎯⎯⎯⎯

Manufacturer ⎯⎯⎯⎯⎯⎯⎯⎯⎯⎯⎯

Cost per yard ⎯⎯⎯⎯⎯⎯⎯⎯⎯⎯⎯

Date purchased ⎯⎯⎯⎯⎯⎯⎯⎯⎯⎯

Notes ⎯⎯⎯⎯⎯⎯⎯⎯⎯⎯⎯

⎯⎯⎯⎯⎯⎯⎯⎯⎯⎯⎯⎯⎯⎯⎯⎯

Yardage and Fabric Swatches

Name of fabric _____

Manufacturer _____

Cost per yard _____

Date purchased _____

Notes _____

_____

Name of fabric _____

Manufacturer _____

Cost per yard _____

Date purchased _____

Notes _____

_____

Name of fabric _____

Manufacturer _____

Cost per yard _____

Date purchased _____

Notes _____

_____

Quilt Project Plan

Date _____

Quilt is for: Me _____ To Gift _____ To Sell _____

Recipient, if a gift:_____

Size of quilt:
Baby ___ Lap ___ Twin ___ Queen ___ King ___ Other _____

Pattern name: _____

Colors to use:_____

Pattern to use: _____

Type of batting: _____

How it will be quilted:
By Hand _____
By Machine _____
By Someone Else _____

Notes

_____

_____

_____

_____

_____

_____

_____

Quilt Project Plan - Materials

Fabric

Top

_____

_____

_____

_____

_____

Backing

_____

_____

Binding

_____

Thread

Color _____

Size & Number of Spools _____

Color _____

Size & Number of Spools _____

Color _____

Size & Number of Spools _____

Batting

Size _____

Loft _____

Cotton/Wool/Bamboo/Blend _____

Other Materials

_____

_____

_____

_____

_____

_____

Yardage and Fabric Swatches

Name of fabric _____

Manufacturer _____

Cost per yard _____

Date purchased _____

Notes _____

_____

Name of fabric _____

Manufacturer _____

Cost per yard _____

Date purchased _____

Notes _____

_____

Name of fabric _____

Manufacturer _____

Cost per yard _____

Date purchased _____

Notes _____

_____

Yardage and Fabric Swatches

Name of fabric _____

Manufacturer _____

Cost per yard _____

Date purchased _____

Notes _____

_____

Name of fabric _____

Manufacturer _____

Cost per yard _____

Date purchased _____

Notes _____

_____

Name of fabric _____

Manufacturer _____

Cost per yard _____

Date purchased _____

Notes _____

_____

Yardage and Fabric Swatches

Name of fabric _____

Manufacturer _____

Cost per yard _____

Date purchased _____

Notes _____

_____

Name of fabric _____

Manufacturer _____

Cost per yard _____

Date purchased _____

Notes _____

_____

Name of fabric _____

Manufacturer _____

Cost per yard _____

Date purchased _____

Notes _____

_____

Yardage and Fabric Swatches

Name of fabric _____

Manufacturer _____

Cost per yard _____

Date purchased _____

Notes _____

_____

Name of fabric _____

Manufacturer _____

Cost per yard _____

Date purchased _____

Notes _____

_____

Name of fabric _____

Manufacturer _____

Cost per yard _____

Date purchased _____

Notes _____

_____

Yardage and Fabric Swatches

Name of fabric _____

Manufacturer _____

Cost per yard _____

Date purchased _____

Notes _____

_____

Name of fabric _____

Manufacturer _____

Cost per yard _____

Date purchased _____

Notes _____

_____

Name of fabric _____

Manufacturer _____

Cost per yard _____

Date purchased _____

Notes _____

_____

Yardage and Fabric Swatches

Name of fabric

Manufacturer

Cost per yard

Date purchased

Notes

Name of fabric

Manufacturer

Cost per yard

Date purchased

Notes

Name of fabric

Manufacturer

Cost per yard

Date purchased

Notes

Quilt Project Plan

Date _____

Quilt is for: Me _____ To Gift _____ To Sell _____

Recipient, if a gift:_____

Size of quilt:
Baby ___ Lap ___ Twin ___ Queen ___ King ___ Other _____

Pattern name: _____

Colors to use:_____

Pattern to use: _____

Type of batting: _____

How it will be quilted:
By Hand _____
By Machine _____
By Someone Else _____

Notes

_____
_____
_____
_____
_____
_____
_____

Quilt Project Plan - Materials

Fabric
Top

_____
_____
_____
_____
_____

Backing

_____
_____

Binding

_____

Thread

Color _____
Size & Number of Spools _____

Color _____
Size & Number of Spools _____

Color _____
Size & Number of Spools _____

Batting

Size _____
Loft _____
Cotton/Wool/Bamboo/Blend _____

Other Materials

_____
_____
_____
_____
_____

Yardage and Fabric Swatches

Name of fabric

Manufacturer

Cost per yard

Date purchased

Notes

Name of fabric

Manufacturer

Cost per yard

Date purchased

Notes

Name of fabric

Manufacturer

Cost per yard

Date purchased

Notes

Yardage and Fabric Swatches

Name of fabric

Manufacturer

Cost per yard

Date purchased

Notes

Name of fabric

Manufacturer

Cost per yard

Date purchased

Notes

Name of fabric

Manufacturer

Cost per yard

Date purchased

Notes

Yardage and Fabric Swatches

Name of fabric _____

Manufacturer _____

Cost per yard _____

Date purchased _____

Notes _____

_____

Name of fabric _____

Manufacturer _____

Cost per yard _____

Date purchased _____

Notes _____

_____

Name of fabric _____

Manufacturer _____

Cost per yard _____

Date purchased _____

Notes _____

_____

Yardage and Fabric Swatches

Name of fabric

Manufacturer

Cost per yard

Date purchased

Notes

Name of fabric

Manufacturer

Cost per yard

Date purchased

Notes

Name of fabric

Manufacturer

Cost per yard

Date purchased

Notes

Yardage and Fabric swatches

Name of fabric _____

Manufacturer _____

Cost per yard _____

Date purchased _____

Notes _____

_____

Name of fabric _____

Manufacturer _____

Cost per yard _____

Date purchased _____

Notes _____

_____

Name of fabric _____

Manufacturer _____

Cost per yard _____

Date purchased _____

Notes _____

_____

Yardage and Fabric Swatches

Name of fabric _____

Manufacturer _____

Cost per yard _____

Date purchased _____

Notes _____

_____

Name of fabric _____

Manufacturer _____

Cost per yard _____

Date purchased _____

Notes _____

_____

Name of fabric _____

Manufacturer _____

Cost per yard _____

Date purchased _____

Notes _____

_____

Quilt Project Plan

Date _____

Quilt is for: Me _____ To Gift _____ To Sell _____

Recipient, if a gift:_____

Size of quilt:
Baby ____ Lap ____ Twin ____ Queen ____ King ____ Other _____

Pattern name: _____

Colors to use:_____

Pattern to use: _____

Type of batting: _____

How it will be quilted:
By Hand _____
By Machine _____
By Someone Else _____

Notes

_____

_____

_____

_____

_____

_____

_____

Quilt Project Plan - Materials

Fabric

Top

_____

_____

_____

_____

_____

Backing

_____

_____

Binding

_____

Thread

Color _____

Size & Number of Spools _____

Color _____

Size & Number of Spools _____

Color _____

Size & Number of Spools _____

Batting

Size _____

Loft _____

Cotton/Wool/Bamboo/Blend _____

Other Materials

_____

_____

_____

_____

_____

_____

Yardage and Fabric Swatches

Name of fabric _____

Manufacturer _____

Cost per yard _____

Date purchased _____

Notes _____

_____

Name of fabric _____

Manufacturer _____

Cost per yard _____

Date purchased _____

Notes _____

_____

Name of fabric _____

Manufacturer _____

Cost per yard _____

Date purchased _____

Notes _____

_____

Yardage and Fabric Swatches

Name of fabric _____

Manufacturer _____

Cost per yard _____

Date purchased _____

Notes _____

_____

Name of fabric _____

Manufacturer _____

Cost per yard _____

Date purchased _____

Notes _____

_____

Name of fabric _____

Manufacturer _____

Cost per yard _____

Date purchased _____

Notes _____

_____

Yardage and Fabric Swatches

Name of fabric _____

Manufacturer _____

Cost per yard _____

Date purchased _____

Notes _____

_____

Name of fabric _____

Manufacturer _____

Cost per yard _____

Date purchased _____

Notes _____

_____

Name of fabric _____

Manufacturer _____

Cost per yard _____

Date purchased _____

Notes _____

_____

Yardage and Fabric Swatches

Name of fabric

Manufacturer

Cost per yard

Date purchased

Notes

Name of fabric

Manufacturer

Cost per yard

Date purchased

Notes

Name of fabric

Manufacturer

Cost per yard

Date purchased

Notes

Yardage and Fabric Swatches

Name of fabric _____

Manufacturer _____

Cost per yard _____

Date purchased _____

Notes _____

_____

Name of fabric _____

Manufacturer _____

Cost per yard _____

Date purchased _____

Notes _____

_____

Name of fabric _____

Manufacturer _____

Cost per yard _____

Date purchased _____

Notes _____

_____

Yardage and Fabric Swatches

Name of fabric _____

Manufacturer _____

Cost per yard _____

Date purchased _____

Notes _____

_____

Name of fabric _____

Manufacturer _____

Cost per yard _____

Date purchased _____

Notes _____

_____

Name of fabric _____

Manufacturer _____

Cost per yard _____

Date purchased _____

Notes _____

_____

Quilt Project Plan

Date _____

Quilt is for: Me _____ To Gift _____ To Sell _____

Recipient, if a gift:_____

Size of quilt:
Baby ____ Lap ____ Twin ____ Queen ____ King ____ Other _____

Pattern name: _____

Colors to use:_____

Pattern to use: _____

Type of batting: _____

How it will be quilted:
By Hand _____
By Machine _____
By Someone Else _____

Notes

_____

_____

_____

_____

_____

_____

_____

Quilt Project Plan - Materials

Fabric

Top

_____

_____

_____

_____

_____

Backing

_____

_____

Binding

_____

Thread

Color _____

Size & Number of Spools _____

Color _____

Size & Number of Spools _____

Color _____

Size & Number of Spools _____

Batting

Size _____

Loft _____

Cotton/Wool/Bamboo/Blend _____

Other Materials

_____

_____

_____

_____

_____

_____

Yardage and Fabric Swatches

Name of fabric _____

Manufacturer _____

Cost per yard _____

Date purchased _____

Notes _____

_____

Name of fabric _____

Manufacturer _____

Cost per yard _____

Date purchased _____

Notes _____

_____

Name of fabric _____

Manufacturer _____

Cost per yard _____

Date purchased _____

Notes _____

_____

Yardage and Fabric Swatches

Name of fabric

Manufacturer

Cost per yard

Date purchased

Notes

Name of fabric

Manufacturer

Cost per yard

Date purchased

Notes

Name of fabric

Manufacturer

Cost per yard

Date purchased

Notes

Yardage and Fabric Swatches

Name of fabric _____

Manufacturer _____

Cost per yard _____

Date purchased _____

Notes _____

_____

Name of fabric _____

Manufacturer _____

Cost per yard _____

Date purchased _____

Notes _____

_____

Name of fabric _____

Manufacturer _____

Cost per yard _____

Date purchased _____

Notes _____

_____

Yardage and Fabric Swatches

Name of fabric

Manufacturer

Cost per yard

Date purchased

Notes

Name of fabric

Manufacturer

Cost per yard

Date purchased

Notes

Name of fabric

Manufacturer

Cost per yard

Date purchased

Notes

Yardage and Fabric Swatches

Name of fabric _____

Manufacturer _____

Cost per yard _____

Date purchased _____

Notes _____

_____

Name of fabric _____

Manufacturer _____

Cost per yard _____

Date purchased _____

Notes _____

_____

Name of fabric _____

Manufacturer _____

Cost per yard _____

Date purchased _____

Notes _____

_____

Yardage and Fabric Swatches

Name of fabric _____

Manufacturer _____

Cost per yard _____

Date purchased _____

Notes _____

_____

Name of fabric _____

Manufacturer _____

Cost per yard _____

Date purchased _____

Notes _____

_____

Name of fabric _____

Manufacturer _____

Cost per yard _____

Date purchased _____

Notes _____

_____

Quilt Project Plan

Date _____

Quilt is for: Me _____ To Gift _____ To Sell _____

Recipient, if a gift:_____

Size of quilt:
Baby ____ Lap ____ Twin ____ Queen ____ King ____ Other _____

Pattern name: _____

Colors to use:_____

Pattern to use: _____

Type of batting: _____

How it will be quilted:
By Hand _____
By Machine _____
By Someone Else _____

Notes

_____

_____

_____

_____

_____

_____

_____

Quilt Project Plan - Materials

Fabric
Top

_____

_____

_____

_____

_____

Backing

_____

_____

Binding

_____

Thread

Color _____

Size & Number of Spools _____

Color _____

Size & Number of Spools _____

Color _____

Size & Number of Spools _____

Batting

Size _____

Loft _____

Cotton/Wool/Bamboo/Blend _____

Other Materials

_____

_____

_____

_____

_____

_____

Yardage and Fabric Swatches

Name of fabric _____

Manufacturer _____

Cost per yard _____

Date purchased _____

Notes _____

_____

Name of fabric _____

Manufacturer _____

Cost per yard _____

Date purchased _____

Notes _____

_____

Name of fabric _____

Manufacturer _____

Cost per yard _____

Date purchased _____

Notes _____

_____

Yardage and Fabric Swatches

Name of fabric ....

Manufacturer ....

Cost per yard ....

Date purchased ....

Notes ....

....

Name of fabric ....

Manufacturer ....

Cost per yard ....

Date purchased ....

Notes ....

....

Name of fabric ....

Manufacturer ....

Cost per yard ....

Date purchased ....

Notes ....

....

Yardage and Fabric Swatches

Name of fabric _____

Manufacturer _____

Cost per yard _____

Date purchased _____

Notes _____

_____

Name of fabric _____

Manufacturer _____

Cost per yard _____

Date purchased _____

Notes _____

_____

Name of fabric _____

Manufacturer _____

Cost per yard _____

Date purchased _____

Notes _____

_____

Yardage and Fabric Swatches

Name of fabric

Manufacturer

Cost per yard

Date purchased

Notes

Name of fabric

Manufacturer

Cost per yard

Date purchased

Notes

Name of fabric

Manufacturer

Cost per yard

Date purchased

Notes

Yardage and Fabric Swatches

Name of fabric _____

Manufacturer _____

Cost per yard _____

Date purchased _____

Notes _____

_____

Name of fabric _____

Manufacturer _____

Cost per yard _____

Date purchased _____

Notes _____

_____

Name of fabric _____

Manufacturer _____

Cost per yard _____

Date purchased _____

Notes _____

_____

Yardage and Fabric Swatches

Name of fabric

Manufacturer

Cost per yard

Date purchased

Notes

Name of fabric

Manufacturer

Cost per yard

Date purchased

Notes

Name of fabric

Manufacturer

Cost per yard

Date purchased

Notes

Quilt Project Plan

Date _____

Quilt is for: Me _____ To Gift _____ To Sell _____

Recipient, if a gift:_____

Size of quilt:
Baby ___ Lap ___ Twin ___ Queen ___ King ___ Other _____

Pattern name: _____

Colors to use:_____

Pattern to use: _____

Type of batting: _____

How it will be quilted:
By Hand _____
By Machine _____
By Someone Else _____

Notes

_____

_____

_____

_____

_____

_____

_____

Quilt Project Plan - Materials

Fabric

Top

_____
_____
_____
_____
_____

Backing

_____
_____

Binding

_____

Thread

Color _____
Size & Number of Spools _____

Color _____
Size & Number of Spools _____

Color _____
Size & Number of Spools _____

Batting

Size _____
Loft _____
Cotton/Wool/Bamboo/Blend _____

Other Materials

_____
_____
_____
_____
_____
_____

Yardage and Fabric Swatches

Name of fabric _____

Manufacturer _____

Cost per yard _____

Date purchased _____

Notes _____

_____

Name of fabric _____

Manufacturer _____

Cost per yard _____

Date purchased _____

Notes _____

_____

Name of fabric _____

Manufacturer _____

Cost per yard _____

Date purchased _____

Notes _____

_____

Yardage and Fabric Swatches

Name of fabric _____

Manufacturer _____

Cost per yard _____

Date purchased _____

Notes _____

_____

Name of fabric _____

Manufacturer _____

Cost per yard _____

Date purchased _____

Notes _____

_____

Name of fabric _____

Manufacturer _____

Cost per yard _____

Date purchased _____

Notes _____

_____

Yardage and Fabric Swatches

Name of fabric _____

Manufacturer _____

Cost per yard _____

Date purchased _____

Notes _____

_____

Name of fabric _____

Manufacturer _____

Cost per yard _____

Date purchased _____

Notes _____

_____

Name of fabric _____

Manufacturer _____

Cost per yard _____

Date purchased _____

Notes _____

_____

Yardage and Fabric Swatches

Name of fabric _____

Manufacturer _____

Cost per yard _____

Date purchased _____

Notes _____

_____

Name of fabric _____

Manufacturer _____

Cost per yard _____

Date purchased _____

Notes _____

_____

Name of fabric _____

Manufacturer _____

Cost per yard _____

Date purchased _____

Notes _____

_____

Yardage and Fabric Swatches

Name of fabric

Manufacturer

Cost per yard

Date purchased

Notes

Name of fabric

Manufacturer

Cost per yard

Date purchased

Notes

Name of fabric

Manufacturer

Cost per yard

Date purchased

Notes

Yardage and Fabric Swatches

Name of fabric _____

Manufacturer _____

Cost per yard _____

Date purchased _____

Notes _____

_____

Name of fabric _____

Manufacturer _____

Cost per yard _____

Date purchased _____

Notes _____

_____

Name of fabric _____

Manufacturer _____

Cost per yard _____

Date purchased _____

Notes _____

_____

Quilt Projects Record

Quilt name _____

Date top started _____

Date top completed _____

By whom/how was it quilted

_____

Date completed _____

Photo

Quilt Projects Record

Quilt name _____

Date top started _____

Date top completed _____

By whom/how was it quilted

_____

Date completed _____

Photo

Quilt Projects Record

Quilt name _____

Date top started _____

Date top completed _____

By whom/how was it quilted

_____

Date completed _____

Photo

Quilt Projects Record

Quilt name _____

Date top started _____

Date top completed _____

By whom/how was it quilted

_____

Date completed _____

Photo

Quilt Projects Record

Quilt name _____

Date top started _____

Date top completed _____

By whom/how was it quilted

_____

Date completed _____

Photo

Quilt Projects Record

Quilt name _____

Date top started _____

Date top completed _____

By whom/how was it quilted

_____

Date completed _____

Photo

Quilt Projects Record

Quilt name _____

Date top started _____

Date top completed _____

By whom/how was it quilted

_____

Date completed _____

Photo

Quilt Projects Record

Quilt name _____

Date top started _____

Date top completed _____

By whom/how was it quilted

_____

Date completed _____

Photo

Quilt Projects Record

Quilt name _____

Date top started _____

Date top completed _____

By whom/how was it quilted

_____

Date completed _____

Photo

Quilt Projects Record

Quilt name _____

Date top started _____

Date top completed _____

By whom/how was it quilted

_____

Date completed _____

Photo

Quilt Projects Record

Quilt name _____

Date top started _____

Date top completed _____

By whom/how was it quilted

_____

Date completed _____

Photo

Quilt Projects Record

Quilt name _____

Date top started _____

Date top completed _____

By whom/how was it quilted

_____

Date completed _____

Photo

Quilt Projects Record

Quilt name _____

Date top started _____

Date top completed _____

By whom/how was it quilted

_____

Date completed _____

Photo

Quilt Projects Record

Quilt name _____

Date top started _____

Date top completed _____

By whom/how was it quilted

_____

Date completed _____

Photo

Quilt Projects Record

Quilt name _____

Date top started _____

Date top completed _____

By whom/how was it quilted

_____

Date completed _____

Photo

Quilt Projects Record

Quilt name _____

Date top started _____

Date top completed _____

By whom/how was it quilted

_____

Date completed _____

Photo

Quilt Projects Record

Quilt name _____

Date top started _____

Date top completed _____

By whom/how was it quilted

_____

Date completed _____

Photo

Quilt Projects Record

Quilt name _____

Date top started _____

Date top completed _____

By whom/how was it quilted

_____

Date completed _____

Photo

Notes

Notes

Notes

Notes

Made in the USA
Middletown, DE
18 February 2022